Cowboys

Written and planned by
Nora Stein

Managing Editor
Mary Tapissier

Factual adviser
Frederick Nolan

Cover designer
Patrick Frean

Production
John Morton

Illustrators
Kim Blundell
pages 8,18,24,25,30,31,42,46
Anna Kostal
pages 9,12,13,28,29,38,39,43
W. Francis Phillipps
pages 4-7,10,11,14-17,19-23,27,32-37,
40,41,44,45

Stories and poems
Robert P. Tristram Coffin
Pages 24-25 Old Blue
©1955 by the Administrators of
the Estate of Robert P. Tristram
Coffin. First published in *The
Georgia Review.*
Will C. Brown
Pages 30-31 Trail Man's Bluff
©Will C. Brown

Teacher panel
Susan Bibbings
Netta Christopher
Steve Harley

Project page 28 tested by
Class 1 C, Campsbourne Junior School

First Published 1978
Macdonald Educational Ltd
Holywell House
Worship Street
London EC2

© Macdonald Educational Ltd 1978

ISBN 0 356 054450 0

Printed and bound by
New Interlitho, Milan, Italy

Contents

Cowboys

Macdonald Educational

The Cowboy and His Gear

batwing chaps were easy to snap on

woolly chaps were warm in winter but soggy and smelly when wet

work boots and spurs

Cowboys needed comfortable, hard wearing clothing and gear since they worked outdoors in all sorts of weather. They spent most of their lives in the saddle, so good horse were very important too.

A cowboy's gear had to be comfortable for his horse as well as for himself. A horse in pain would not serve its rider well. The saddle and bit had to fit correctly. Many cowboys did not wear spurs, and those who did filed the points blunt. A good horse needed no more than a little spurring.

Most cowboys spent a lot of money on their saddles and boots. The boots' high heels helped a rider's foot stay in the stirrup. But the pointed toe allowed the rider to pull his foot free if he was thrown. The boots were comfortable in the saddle but crippling to walk in!

Chaps were really leather overalls that shielded the legs. They gave protection in a fall or if a horse tried to bite. Few cowboys wore coats and most relied on warm waistcoats instead. The bandana was a shield from the sun or, when tied over the mouth and nose, from snow or dust. It could be used as a towel, sling or bandage or even as a blindfold for a jumpy horse. A hat shaded the eyes from sun and rain, and its brim could be tied down over the ears in cold weather. It was used to carry water and fan a campfire to life too.

A canteen held water which could be scarce on the trail. In a rainstorm the cowboy put on an oilskin slicker. The rope or lariat could be used to rope a steer or a horse, to drag firewood or pull a steer out of a quicksand bog. Although a cowboy was proud of his guns, he rarely used them against another man.

there were many sorts of hats, some with decorative bands or 'bonnet strings' which tied under the chin

History of the Cowboy

Cattle first came to the New World from Spain with Columbus on his second voyage in 1493. The animals thrived and gradually a cattle industry grew up. Spanish priests and monks raised cattle at their missions and taught their Indian slaves to tend the animals. These Indians, called vaqueros, were the first American cowboys.

By the early nineteenth century the missions were making great profits from their trade in hides and tallow from the cattle.

As the cattle ran loose over the plains of Mexico, California and Texas, they developed into the hardy breed that came to be known as the Texas Longhorn.

In the 1820's the Mexican government began to take away the ranches from the Spanish missionaries. In a war in 1846 the United States won this ranch land in southern California and Texas from Mexico. Many animals were killed in the fighting, but when the herds began to recover, a new cattle business got started, mainly in Texas. The new cowboys were the young Americans. Some had come to America from England, Scotland, France and Germany; others were Indians and freed black slaves. They flocked to Texas to do one of the hardest, dirtiest jobs that man has ever known. Most were less than 25 years old – some were only 14 or 15. They made poor wages and sometimes worked 18 hours a day, seven days a week. But still thousands came.

The great era of the cowboy lasted barely 20 years, from the end of the American Civil War in 1865 to the mid-1880's. In that time, about 40,000 cowboys rode the cattle trails of the Great Plains.

The Devil in Texas

tradition:

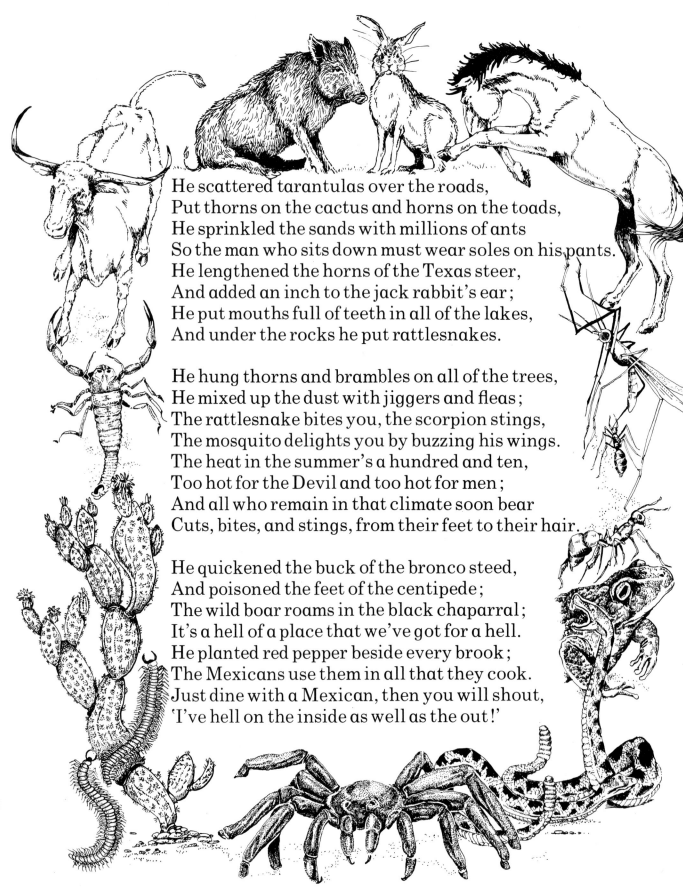

He scattered tarantulas over the roads,
Put thorns on the cactus and horns on the toads,
He sprinkled the sands with millions of ants
So the man who sits down must wear soles on his pants.
He lengthened the horns of the Texas steer,
And added an inch to the jack rabbit's ear;
He put mouths full of teeth in all of the lakes,
And under the rocks he put rattlesnakes.

He hung thorns and brambles on all of the trees,
He mixed up the dust with jiggers and fleas;
The rattlesnake bites you, the scorpion stings,
The mosquito delights you by buzzing his wings.
The heat in the summer's a hundred and ten,
Too hot for the Devil and too hot for men;
And all who remain in that climate soon bear
Cuts, bites, and stings, from their feet to their hair.

He quickened the buck of the bronco steed,
And poisoned the feet of the centipede;
The wild boar roams in the black chaparral;
It's a hell of a place that we've got for a hell.
He planted red pepper beside every brook;
The Mexicans use them in all that they cook.
Just dine with a Mexican, then you will shout,
'I've hell on the inside as well as the out!'

Bucking Bronco

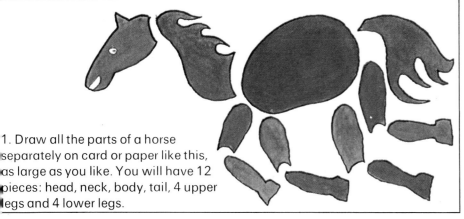

1. Draw all the parts of a horse separately on card or paper like this, as large as you like. You will have 12 pieces: head, neck, body, tail, 4 upper legs and 4 lower legs.

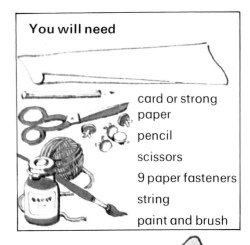

You will need

card or strong paper

pencil

scissors

9 paper fasteners

string

paint and brush

2. Paint the horse and, when it is dry, cut out the pieces.

3. Carefully make holes with a pencil in all the pieces where they will fit together.

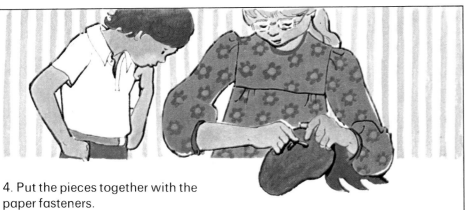

4. Put the pieces together with the paper fasteners.

5. Make a hole at the top of the body and on the neck. Tie a long piece of string into the holes. By jerking the string you can make your horse become a bucking bronco.

The Roundup

In the spring and autumn of every year all the ranches in a district got together and held a roundup. The men gathered all the cattle from the open range and separated and branded them according to which ranch they belonged. In these roundups the cowboys might have to work for as long as 40 days, rounding up cattle that had drifted away. They also found new calves which had to be branded and earmarked.

Each ranch sent several men to a main camp. The bosses worked out detailed plans. Each rider searched a small area for stray cattle. He would then drive all he found to the roundup ground. In half a day seven or eight hundred animals might be gathered. Each rider had six or more horses which he used for different jobs during the roundup. Circle horses, used for gathering the herd, were very strong and did not tire easily. The night horses were even-tempered and surefooted. The reliable cutting horses were used to 'cut' or separate out one animal from a herd, either for branding or transfer into another herd.

The calves and 'mavericks', adult animals which had no brand, would be cut from the herd, roped and thrown. The animal's feet were tied and two men held it down. Another branded it and a fourth man might cut the animal's ear and clip its horns. The animal was also checked for sores and disease and treated. Men working like this could brand about 25 animals an hour.

The branding iron was hot, but the cowboys were careful and quick. Too shallow a brand might disappear, but too deep a brand would harm the animal.

11

Cattle Brands

Each ranch had its own brand so everyone could tell which cattle and horses belonged to the ranch owner. Even the cowboys who could not read knew how to recognise the brand on the side of an animal.

Some brands were letters or numbers. They often represented the name of a ranch or its owner. Other brands were pictures. Here are some real brands from western ranches.

Circle
Half Circle
Double Circle
Tumbling Right R
Tumbling Left R
Crazy R

Triple R
Triple R Connected
Rocking Seven
Running Seven
Swinging Seven
Flying Seven
Bar
Double Bar
Arrow
U.S. Government brand
U.S. Indian brand

Dollar Sign
Tin Cup
Snake
Rocking Chair
Frying Pan
J. H. Barwise's brand
John Adair's brand
Johnson and Homer
Bull Head
Running W
Tumbling Ladder

By looking at the brands above, you should be able to read or guess what these brands stand for. The answers are on page 47.

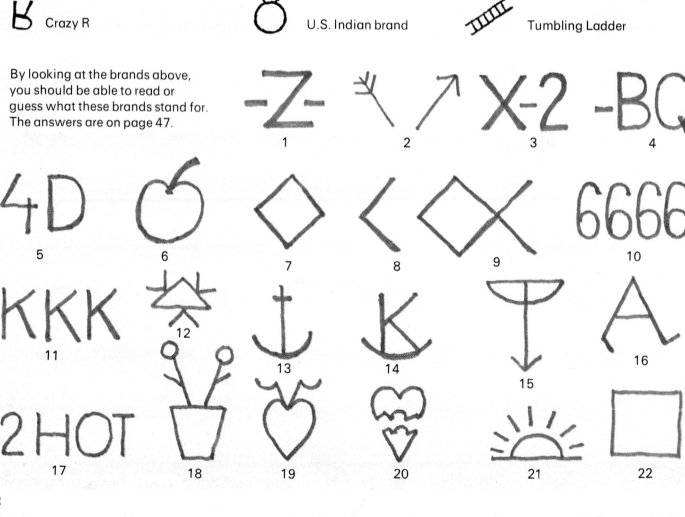

1
2
3
4
5
6
7
8
9
10
11
12
13
14
15
16
17
18
19
20
21
22

Potato Print Branding

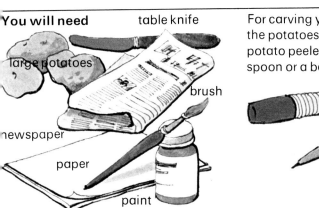

You will need
large potatoes
newspaper
paper
table knife
brush
paint

For carving your brands into the potatoes you could use a potato peeler, the end of a small spoon or a ball point pen.

1. Carefully cut your potato in half with a table knife.

2. Carve your brand into the potato. If it has letters or numbers, do them backwards like mirror writing.

3. You can carve your brand into the potato or carve away the potato around your brand.

4. Brush paint evenly over the potato brand.

5. Lay down newspaper over your work surface. You can print your brands on plain paper, or draw and cut out big pictures of steers or horses and brand them.

The Ranch

Many ranches began as settlements of tents or covered wagons. If the owner was prosperous, the settlement might expand to a ranch like this, with good pasture, living quarters for the family, bunkhouses for the cowhands, a cookhouse, blacksmith's shop and sheds.

Conditions in the bunk house for the cowboys were always rugged. What attracted a cowboy to a ranch was not his lodgings but rather the horses he was offered. Usually a cowboy had a string of six or seven horses which only he worked and cared for. The string was calle a remuda. Some of the horses were well-trained. Two or three would be half wild and used only on short rides. A cowboy knew he was being asked to leave the ranch if his horses were taken away from him.

In the summer there were many jobs on the ranch and range. Cattle and horses had to be tended. The range had to be carefully watched for fire in dry weather, and there were repairs around the ranch and sometimes farm chores too. In the winter life was much slower. Two out of three ranch hands were laid off until the spring roundup and cattle drives began. Some men took jobs bartending or blacksmithing if they were lucky enough to find them. Others rode from ranch to ranch doing odd jobs in exchange for a meal. Those who did stay at a ranch worked mostly at maintenance, collecting firewood and making sure that cattle did not freeze or starve to death on the range.

For all his work, a cowboy might be paid $40 a month.

Cattle Barons and Business

The growth of the cattle business was spurred on by the great demand for cattle by the stockyards in the north of the United States. Cowboys drove thousands of animals up the cattle trails to railway depots from which the animals were shipped to these yards.

By 1880 cattle had become the biggest business in the West. Fewer than 50 men controlled more than eight million hectares of western prairie land on which 12 million cattle grazed. These men who made their fortunes from the cattle business were called cattle barons. Some began as ranch hands and gradually rounded up their own small herds of wild cattle, mavericks or strays whose brands they altered. With luck, their fortunes grew. One cattle baron who began as a cowboy was Charlie Goodnight.

Goodnight ruthlessly drove Indians and other settlers from the land and water he wanted and replaced the roaming buffalo with his herds. He persuaded investors to back him, and in five years he had more than 100,000 head of cattle. He sold 30,000 animals to the eastern beef markets for half a million dollars every year. But most cattle barons had no idea how to ride, brand or shoot. Many were just businessmen who invested their money in livestock.

They built grand houses on the prairies and lived in luxury. Very often their wives were the only women around for miles. These women sometimes helped their husbands to manage their ranches and finances. Even when cowboys did not like their bosses, they usually had great respect for the cattle barons' wives.

The Railroad Corral

traditional

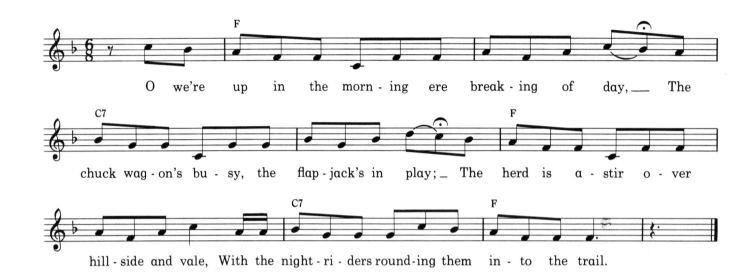

O we're up in the morn-ing ere break-ing of day, — The
chuck wag-on's bu-sy, the flap-jack's in play; — The herd is a-stir o-ver
hill-side and vale, With the night-ri-ders round-ing them in-to the trail.

So come take up your cinches, come shake out your reins,
Come wake your old bronco and break for the plains,
Come roust out your steers from the long chapparal,
For the outfit is off to the railroad corral.

The sun circles upward. The steers as they plod,
Are pounding to powder the hot prairie sod,
And it seems when the dust makes you dizzy and sick,
That we'll never reach noon and the cool, shady crick.

But tie up your handkerchief, play up your nag,
Come dry up your grumbles and try not to lag,
Drive up your steers from the long chapparal,
For we're far on the road to the railroad corral.

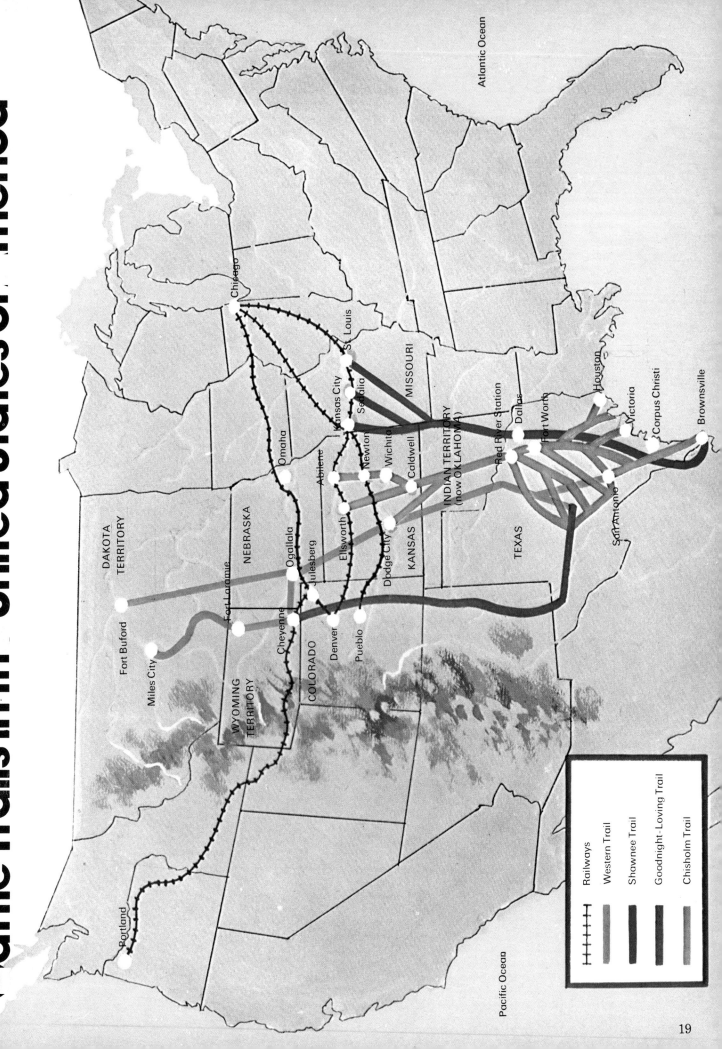

Cattle Trails in the United States of America

Atlantic Ocean

Chicago

St. Louis

MISSOURI

Houston

Kansas City

Sedalia

Newton

Wichita

Caldwell

INDIAN TERRITORY
(now OKLAHOMA)

Red River Station

Dallas

Fort Worth

Victoria

Corpus Christi

Brownsville

Omaha

Abilene

Ellsworth

Dodge City

KANSAS

TEXAS

San Antonio

DAKOTA
TERRITORY

NEBRASKA

Ogallala

Fort Laramie

Julesberg

COLORADO

Cheyenne

Denver

Pueblo

Fort Buford

Miles City

WYOMING
TERRITORY

Portland

Pacific Ocean

Railways

Western Trail

Shawnee Trail

Goodnight-Loving Trail

Chisholm Trail

19

Cattle Drives

The long cattle drive was the most important, exciting and miserable part of the cowboy's job. Most of the drives followed the great cattle trails, the Shawnee, Western, Chisholm and Goodnight-Loving. The last two were named after the men who forged them. The trails led from Texas to the railway depots in Kansas and Missouri which linked the beef business to the East. A steer worth $4 in Texas might fetch $20 up north.

Usually one cowhand was hired for each 300 head of cattle. The herds might range in size from 500 to 15,000 animals. They were walked up to 1600 kilometres on a journey that might last three to four months. An ordinary cowboy earned about $40 per month plus his keep. At the end of a drive his wages would buy him no more than a new suit of clothes and a saddle. The trail boss, or foreman, made much more, about $125 per month. He carried all the responsibility for getting the cattle safely to market. An important part of his job was to scout ahead for good water and resting places and to head off any danger. The cook earned something in between the cowboy's and foreman's wages. A happy drive depended greatly on his good cooking and cheerfulness.

The cowboys often had help from a steer which took a natural lead in the herd. A steer like this would be brought home instead of being sold. One such animal, Old Blue, belonged to Charlie Goodnight and made the journey to Dodge City eight times. He wore a bell around his neck which the other cattle learned to follow.

If a drive went very well, there might be no more trouble than Indians demanding a toll of steers for crossing their land. But often the drives were more difficult and dangerous.

21

Stampede!

Most cattle drives ran into trouble and danger along the route. Hundreds of cattle might be lost. All too often a young cowboy might perish as well – killed by Indians or more likely trampled to death in a stampede.

Longhorns easily panicked and stampeded. The worst stampedes were at night. The herd could be set off by strange noises or smells or any sort of surprise. The cowboys had to keep their camps very orderly and calm.

Sometimes the cowboys' horses might stampede too. Still, the men worried little about the danger to themselves. Their main concerns were lost or injured animals and the precious time spent in rounding up the herd again.

Electrical storms with thunder, lightning and hailstones probably caused more stampedes than anything else. Some stampedes were caused by people. The distant boom of dynamite blasting for a new railway might begin a stampede. One stampede was begun by a woman waving a sunbonnet to chase cattle off her garden. Even the flash of a lantern at night could set them off.

But not all stampedes were accidents. Indians and other rustlers who wanted to steal cattle often ran through the camps shooting, yelling and waving blankets. In the confusion that followed, the rustlers made off with as many animals as they could.

There were other dangers too. In a long drought cattle might die of thirst or starvation. But bad water could kill them as well. Although cattle and horses could swim, river crossings were dangerous. Most cowboys could not swim and many were drowned in floods and panics. Another river hazard was the quicksand on the banks in which animals might become helplessly stuck.

Old Blue

by Robert P. Tristram Coffin

Old Blue was tough
As steers can be,
He could walk from Texas
To eternity.

Mean eye, mean horn,
Bony as death,
He could walk the coyotes
Out of breath.

Bronze at his nose,
Iron at his tail,
Each year he walked
The Chisholm Trail.

San Antone
To Kansas or bust,
He churned three long stat
Into dust.

Eight hundred miles
He led the van,
He wore out wolves,
Dust storms, and man.

He led the longhorns
To the Abilene train,
And he alone
Came home again.

Loyal and true
To the wrong lot,
Old Blue was Judas
Iscariot.

He led his kind
To the floor running red,
To the knife in the throat,
The axe in the head.

Old Blue led steers
To Doomsday flood,
His name is written
In his own blood.

25

The Trail Camp

At the end of each long day the cowboys set up camp. Before they could relax, they had to drive the cattle into a close group and make sure the animals lay down for the night. Then the horses were tied up or put into a rope corral. The cook had arrived first, lit a campfire and set up the chuck wagon. When the hungry cowboys came, a hot dinner would be waiting for them.

Most of the cowboys' food was boring. They usually had beans, known as 'pecos strawberries', bacon, which was called 'overland trout', biscuits and coffee. The men rarely got fresh food on the trail. If they were lucky a farmer might give them eggs and vegetables in return for a calf. Once in a while a steer might be slaughtered and dinner would be a speciality called sonofagun stew. But it was unusual to kill an animal on the trail as most of the meat would go bad before it could be eaten.

After dinner the men sat around the campfire telling jokes and stories. Then they got their bedrolls from the chuck wagon and bedded down. The cook's last job was to point the chuck wagon towards the north so everyone knew which way to head in the morning. Two men stayed up to do the first watch from ten until midnight. They kept the cattle calm by singing lullabies and listened for any disturbances such as Indians or rustlers. There were two more watches during the night. The men knew when to change guard by watching the position of the stars.

Everyone was up at sunrise. Some of the horses in the remuda were only half-broken, and each morning they would have to get used to being ridden again. A ruined breakfast could be the result!

Chuck Wagon

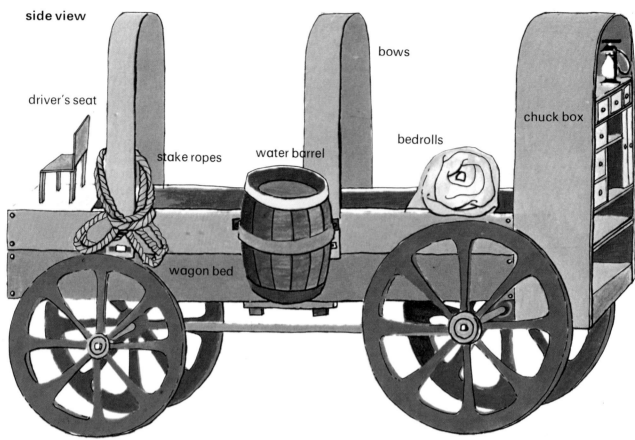

side view

driver's seat

bows

stake ropes

water barrel

bedrolls

chuck box

wagon bed

These are some of the things that you will find in a chuck wagon.

Chuck Box and Boot
flour
sugar
dried fruit
coffee beans
pinto beans
plates, cups
silverware
castor oil
calomel
bandages
needle, thread
razor, strap
salt
lard
baking soda
vinegar
chewing tobacco
rolling tobacco
sourdough keg
matches

molasses
coffeepot
whiskey
skillets
dutch ovens
pot hooks

Wagon Bed
bedrolls
oilskins
corral rope
guns, ammunition
lantern, kerosene
axle grease
extra wagon wheel
salt pork
raw beef
grain for horses
onions, potatoes

Tool Box
shovel
axe
branding irons
horseshoeing equipment
extra skillets

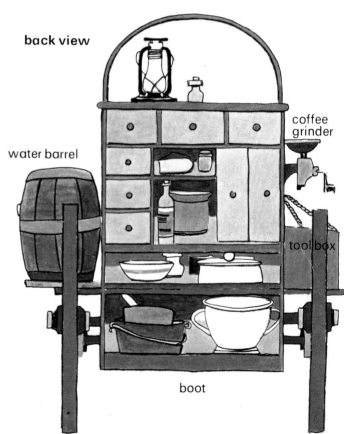

back view

water barrel

coffee grinder

tool box

boot

You will need

strawboard, cane or wire

paints and brushes

yogurt pot

paper fasteners

glue

pins

lots of cardboard boxes large and small

scissors

tape

stapler

fabric

paper

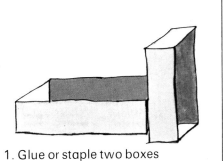

1. Glue or staple two boxes together like this for the chuck wagon's body.

2. Make three bows from strawboard, cane or wire. Staple or glue them on.

3. Make shelves, cupboards and drawers from small boxes. Use paper fasteners for handles.

4. Glue on a yogurt pot water barrel, paper coffee grinder, tool box and lantern.

5. Pin on wheels made from card or cheese boxes.

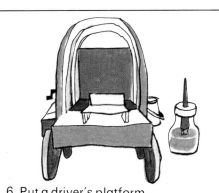

6. Put a driver's platform and a seat at the front.

7. Paint the chuck wagon. Let it dry.

8. Pin fabric over the bows for a covering.

9. Fill the chuck wagon with bedrolls and food provisions for a long drive.

Trail Man's Bluff

by Will C. Brown

This rider, Joe Canady, hung around my chuck wagon, waiting for Witherspoon to come back from the river, and I took a liking to him. He kept his eyes and nose trained on the sonofagun stew I had simmering and asked when we aimed to ford.

"Early in the morning," I said, punching up the fire. "Least, that's Grober's plans."

"Grober?"

"Luke Grober, our foreman. The riders have got other names for him. He was hired to boss this drive, and that's his strong suit—bossin'."

The Witherspoon trail herd was a big one—two thousand head of crazy longhorns. They moved like they had decided unanimous to buck every dogged inch of the distance to the Kansas market. The riders were raw-frazzled, even before we got to the Red River.

About sundown, Mr. Witherspoon rode back to the night camp and said the river was up and half a mile wide at Roan's Crossing. Then I knew the fording was going to be the devil's own problem.

Grober rode in. He was a new man Witherspoon had signed on at Santone to run the drive and he wore his authority all over him, like a poncho. I was thankful I was only the cook and wouldn't be under his orders when it came time to try the crossing.

Our outfit was from down south, on the Salado, and we never had attempted a river fording as wide as this one. The Red River was something to make a trail boss gnaw his stirrups.

Canady waited until Witherspoon and Grober turned and noticed him. Then I saw a funny thing. Grober bit off whatever he was saying. For just a second I got the impression the swarthy trail boss wanted to go for his leg gun.

"This here's a rider name of Joe Canady," I said. "He's looking to sign on with a trail crew going north."

Witherspoon had nothing on his mind but the fording. He dragged a slow look over Canady, and said, "Grober's doing the hiring on this drive."

Canady's mild expression remained. "Maybe we've met before, Grober."

Grober said, "Hell, I can't remember every tramp rider in Texas. . . . We got a full crew."

He turned and stalked over to the riders. You could hear him giving sharp orders for the night guard and telling them we forded at daylight.

Canady stood where he was planted. I saw his mouth tighten in a kind of smile. He said, "No. Not at daylight."

I poked out a plate of stew and beans and biscuits to Canady. He squatted and ate it. Then he rode off.

But when I got the wagon loaded next morning and drove to the river, there was Canady, sitting a good piece of horse-flesh.

Witherspoon joined us, and Canady spoke politely. "Your herd won't cross, Mr. Witherspoon. Somebody's not going at this right."

Witherspoon frowned. "You ever know Grober before, somewhere?"

"I knew a man once by that name.

Lost my stake to him in a poker game. I found out later the deck was peculiar. Lost my herd and had to move on."

Witherspoon turned that over. "You want to claim Grober cheated you? You want to make trouble over it?"

Canady looked him in the eye. "I was a grown man, and gambling with a stranger was my own fault. I just want a job."

But now the lead animals of the herd were coming down the slope below us, to the water. I could see Grober galloping back and forth on the flanks, yelling orders. Then the trouble started.

Those first mosshorns got no more than a knee wet when they came to a full balk. They wouldn't swim. The lead critters dodged back, panicky. Above all the noise Grober was yelling and eating out the riders. But the cattle jammed up in the edge of the river.

"Keep proddin' 'em!" Witherspoon yelled. "Dammit, keep proddin'!"

The riders whooped and charged, and ropes popped against hides like bullets, but in spite of all anybody could do, the jam was getting worse and we were risking losing some cattle.

After a while the men had to give up and let the herd drift back to the first grass.

Grober rode up. He was dirt-covered, mad and breathing hard. He cussed the longhorns and he cussed

30

the men. When he simmered down a little, Mr. Witherspoon said, "This man Canady, here, said those cattle wouldn't cross. Maybe he knows a better way."

"If he's so damn good, maybe he'd like to take over," snapped Grober.

"Well, I hadn't figured to take over as foreman," Canady said. "But I do need to get to Kansas. I could sure use a foreman's pay on this drive."

"All right!" Witherspoon exploded. "How in hell would *you* do it?"

"Not being on your payroll yet," Canady said reluctantly, "I'd hesitate to tell Mr. Grober his business."

"Damn it, man!" Witherspoon snapped. "We got to get those longhorns across! If you know how to do it, you're foreman for the trip!"

That hit Grober. He nodded and sneered. "All right, Canady, you do it. I'll turn 'em over to you and take a rider's shift. Let's see you cross 'em!"

I had sure seen a man's bluff called. If Canady could do something with that herd it was going to surprise me.

Canady said, "My gear's cached upriver. When I get back, we'll ford."

Witherspoon roared out, wanting to know what his gear had to do with crossing the Red River.

"You want me to get 'em across?" Canady's voice was edgy. He loped off.

Some of the riders had come up and were taking it in. Grober's mouth was tight set. He said that'd be the last we'd see of that bluffing trail tramp.

But when the sun was two-thirds to noon, Canady came back. He unloaded

his warbag to the wagon.

"All right," he said. "Let's ford."

"Spirit finally moved you, has it?" Grober said, sarcastic.

But Witherspoon spoke to the men, and Canady rode off with them.

After a while, we saw them coming. I spotted Canady, with two other riders, prodding the mosshorns.

The first old cows were crowded to the water. They didn't like it, but the riders hazed them on in and the back pressure of the herd began building up on the leaders, just like it had been that morning.

Then it was like magic. Those crazy longhorns struck out swimming.

The whole river seemed to fill up with cow heads and floating horns. Canady and the lead riders swam their horses right along with them, and at last the first animals were across to the far bank. The main herd was strung out behind them. Finally, the drags came along, and I knew the crossing was made.

That night we pitched camp well up in the Territory. When Canady gave his orders for the night guard, Grober was polite as a preacher and the men were grinning. They all knew that Canady had laid down higher cards than Grober and that Witherspoon had him a first-class trail boss.

It was late, and just Canady and I were squatting at the dying cook-fire.

"You mind telling me what kind of hoo-doo you worked on them mosshorns?" I asked him.

"No hoo-doo." Canady spoke

quietly. "It's just that your outfit's a South Texas bunch—never had such a wide fording to make before. Also, the river bends above here, runs nearly due north and south where we crossed."

"What's that got to do with it?"

"I could have told Grober right off," he said. "But I figured it was my time to use a stacked deck. I really needed this job. The fording—it's just that we had to drive the cattle east across the river. Straight into the sun. You never ford wide water eastward in the morning or westward in the evening. Cattle won't swim anything they can't see the other side of, and they can't see the other side against a blinding sun."

"So that's why you waited till near noon," I grunted, catching on.

"Yeah. Grober knows cards, but I know cattle . . . This is a good outfit—best trail cooking I ever ate!" He grinned big and then slowly ambled off to his bedroll.

Cattle Towns

Because of the business and people attracted by the new railroads in the 1860's, new towns grew up around the railway depots. They were called cattle towns or cow towns. There the long cattle drives ended and the cattle were sold and shipped east by rail.

After months on the trail, the cowboys were overjoyed when they finally reached town. Sometimes they announced their arrival by yelling and shooting up the streets. Here at last they could have baths, haircuts, change of clothes and a chance to spend their wages in the saloons. For the beef brokers, town was the place to make deals. Millions of animals were bought and sold. The railroad men could load up their empty trains with cattle for the return trip east.

During the cattle season the populations of these tiny towns swelled. The shops, saloons and hotels did big

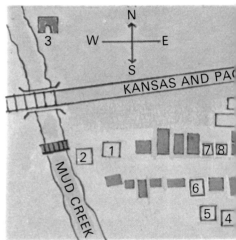

ABILENE 1866: 1. Blockhouse Hotel 2. Wild Bill Hickok's house 3. Tim Hersey's corn mill 4. school 5. church 6. Bull Head Saloon 7. prison 8. McInerney's shoe shop 9. railway depot 10. Alamo Saloon 11. post

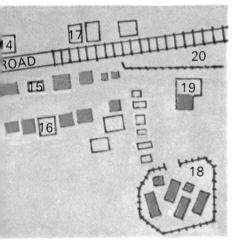

office 12. American Hotel 13. Novelty Theatre 14. Justice Building 15. Pearl Saloon 16. Merchant's Hotel 17. rental stables 18. red light district 19. Drovers Cottage Hotel 20. Great Western stockyards

business. In the winter, when there were no cowboys or businessmen, the saloonkeepers, gamblers and women went to the larger cities. The population was reduced to a few hundred permanent residents. The town became peaceful once more.

Abilene, Kansas was the first great cattle town. It boomed with big business for four years after 1867. Then the railroad was extended west and business moved with it. Abilene was a wild and lawless town, but Dodge City, also in Kansas, was even wilder. It was the last of the cattle towns and thrived for ten years. But some towns flourished for only one year.

Gradually more homesteaders and permanent settlers moved into the towns. These people formed town governments and hired law officers in an effort to make their lives quieter and safer.

The Long Trail

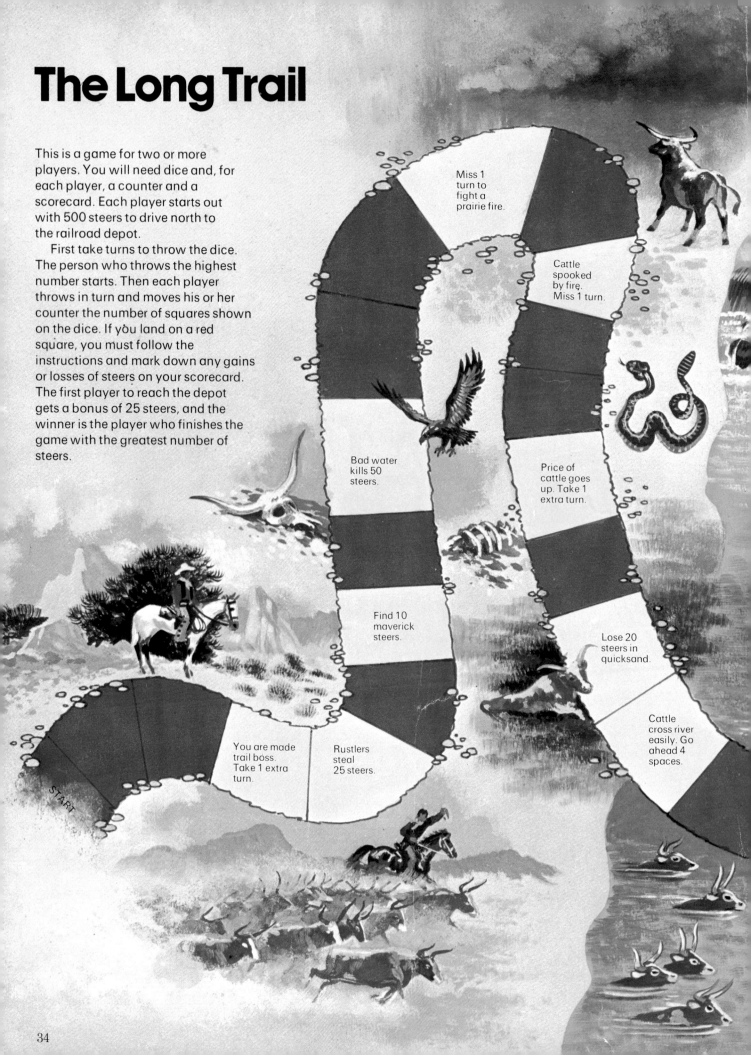

This is a game for two or more players. You will need dice and, for each player, a counter and a scorecard. Each player starts out with 500 steers to drive north to the railroad depot.

First take turns to throw the dice. The person who throws the highest number starts. Then each player throws in turn and moves his or her counter the number of squares shown on the dice. If you land on a red square, you must follow the instructions and mark down any gains or losses of steers on your scorecard. The first player to reach the depot gets a bonus of 25 steers, and the winner is the player who finishes the game with the greatest number of steers.

Miss 1 turn to fight a prairie fire.

Cattle spooked by fire. Miss 1 turn.

Bad water kills 50 steers.

Price of cattle goes up. Take 1 extra turn.

Find 10 maverick steers.

Lose 20 steers in quicksand.

You are made trail boss. Take 1 extra turn.

Rustlers steal 25 steers.

Cattle cross river easily. Go ahead 4 spaces.

START

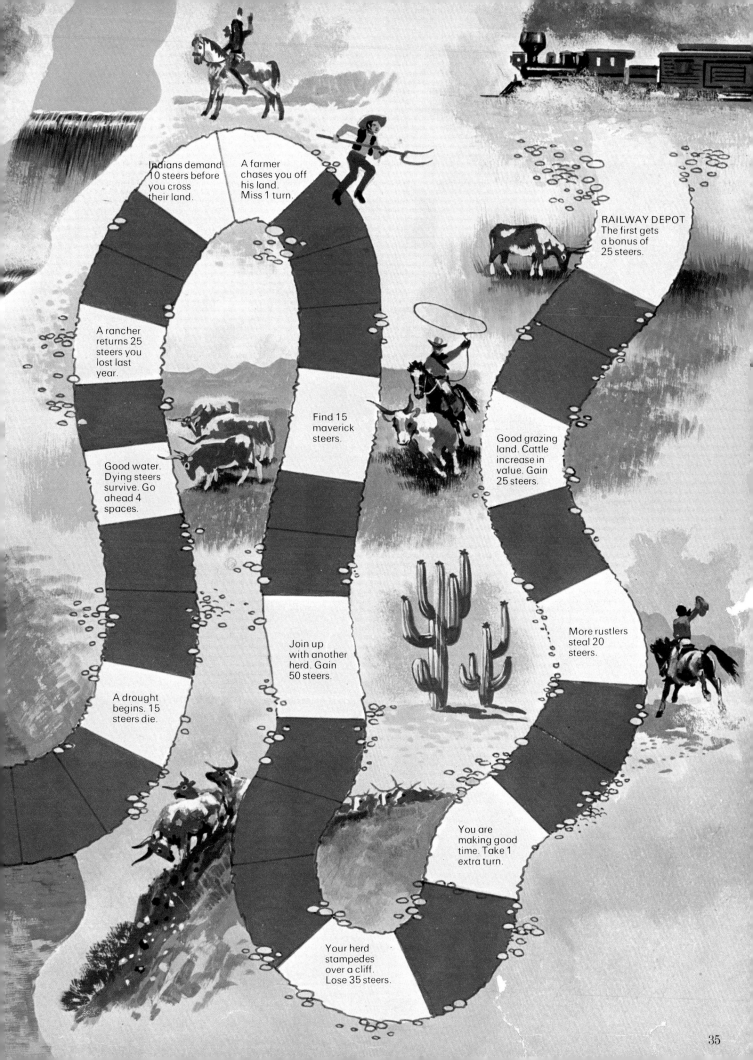

Indians demand 10 steers before you cross their land.

A farmer chases you off his land. Miss 1 turn.

RAILWAY DEPOT
The first gets a bonus of 25 steers.

A rancher returns 25 steers you lost last year.

Find 15 maverick steers.

Good grazing land. Cattle increase in value. Gain 25 steers.

Good water. Dying steers survive. Go ahead 4 spaces.

More rustlers steal 20 steers.

A drought begins. 15 steers die.

Join up with another herd. Gain 50 steers.

You are making good time. Take 1 extra turn.

Your herd stampedes over a cliff. Lose 35 steers.

35

Frontier Town

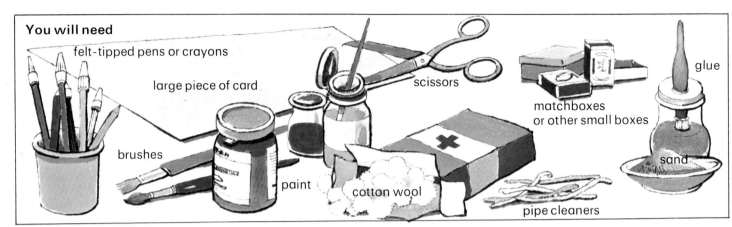

You will need

felt-tipped pens or crayons

large piece of card

brushes

paint

cotton wool

scissors

matchboxes or other small boxes

glue

sand

pipe cleaners

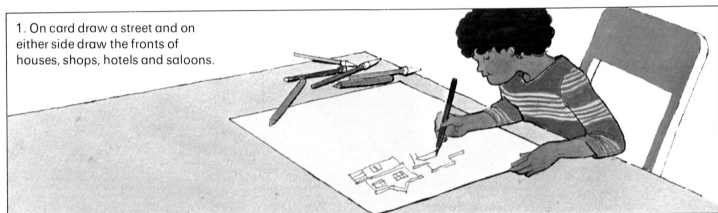

1. On card draw a street and on either side draw the fronts of houses, shops, hotels and saloons.

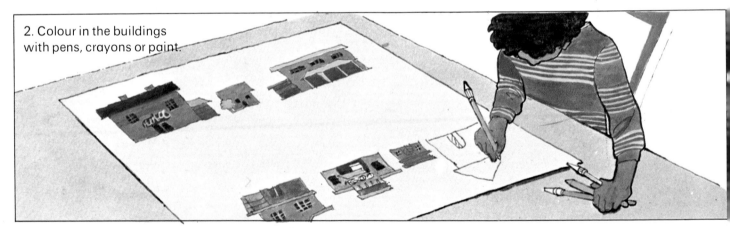

2. Colour in the buildings with pens, crayons or paint.

3. Cut ar
the builc

4. Put boxes behind and tape them to the building fronts. This is just like a real frontier town where the buildings were really shacks with false fronts.

5. Spread glue along the street and sprinkle sand over it. Glue down pieces of painted cotton wool for sagebrush.

You can make cowboys and horses from pipe cleaners and you could add a pipe cleaner corral with steers too.

You could act out a showdown in your town or just an ordinary day – which was very exciting in the Wild West!

We show a small frontier town here, but you could make a large one with a bigger piece of card and shoeboxes instead of small boxes.

Buffalo Bill's Wild West

Buffalo Bill Cody

Cowboys sometimes pretended to be tougher than they really were. They swaggered down the streets but when challenged by the sheriff, meekly handed over their guns. Still, visitors from the East had an image of cowboys as tough and wild. Cowboys began staging fake shootouts and hangings for the visitors.

Soon people were staging shows of cowboy antics. Wild Bill Hickok had a show at Niagara Falls in which he and some Indians and Mexicans roped buffalo for the amusement of the tourists. Buffalo Bill Cody had the most famous of the Wild West shows. It began in 1882 when Cody heard that his hometown had no Independence Day festivities planned. He quickly put together a programme of shooting, riding and bronco busting. After this he organised his 'Wild West'. The show toured the United

States and Europe. Queen Victoria much en...
London.

   In the show Buffalo Bill rode his own b...
horse. Cowboys and Indians did roping and...
Even an attack on a stagecoach by Indians was...
The most exciting shooting was done by a young w...
called Annie Oakley. One of her acts was shooting at...
glass balls that she could see only in a mirror! Annie
Oakley's act started the show. She was supposed to
reassure the women and children in the audience.

   Out of these shows came the rodeos, which are really
contests of skill for cowboys. The word 'rodeo' comes
from the Spanish and means 'roundup'. Wild West shows
have not survived, but many rodeos are still held in the
American West.

Annie Oakley

Billy the Kid

traditional

Billy was a bad man
And carried a big gun,
He was always chasing women
And kept 'em on the run.

He shot men every morning
Just to make a morning meal—
If his gun ran out of bullets
He killed them with cold steel.

He kept folks in hot water,
And he stole from many a stage,
When his gut was full of liquor
He was always in a rage.

But one day he met a man
Who was a whole lot badder—
And now he's dead—
And we ain't none the sadder.

Cowboy Breakfast

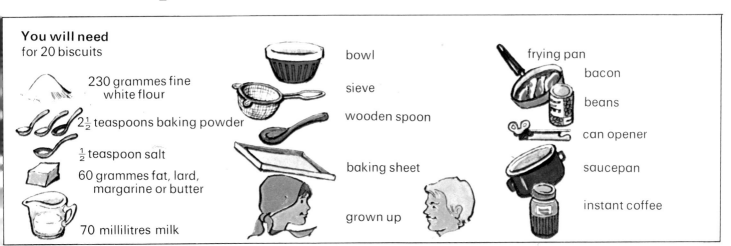

You will need
for 20 biscuits

230 grammes fine white flour

2½ teaspoons baking powder

½ teaspoon salt

60 grammes fat, lard, margarine or butter

70 millilitres milk

bowl

sieve

wooden spoon

baking sheet

grown up

frying pan

bacon

beans

can opener

saucepan

instant coffee

1. Preheat oven to 450°F (230°C or gas mark 6). Sift together 230 grammes flour, ½ teaspoon salt, 2½ teaspoons baking powder in a bowl.

2. With clean fingers, work into the dry ingredients the 60 grammes of fat until the mixture looks like breadcrumbs.

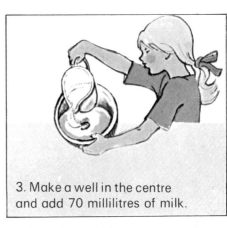

3. Make a well in the centre and add 70 millilitres of milk.

4. Mix for one minute only with a wooden spoon.

5. Drop spoonsful of the dough on to a baking sheet. You should have enough for about 20 biscuits.

6. Bake for 12 to 15 minutes or until browned.

7. Meanwhile, heat the beans, fry the bacon and boil water for coffee.

The Big Die Up

The cold winters and heavy snow in cattle country always caused some deaths in the herds. But most animals could survive the winter if they were in good condition.

The winter of 1886-1887 was the worst anyone could remember. In the spring and summer there had been a terrible drought. Many cattle had died from starvation, drinking putrid water and getting stuck in mud and quicksand. The cattle that survived were thin and weak. Then the terrible cold, unending blizzards and freezing rain struck.

The only hope of saving the cattle was to keep them moving. But they would move only by their own choice. If they did move, the weaklings would soon be left behind. Soon the trail would be littered with bodies of dead animals and perhaps an unfortunate cowboy.

In the winter of 1886-1887 half the cattle on the northern ranges died. The herds in central Texas suffered nearly as much. Whole herds were wiped out together with people's fortunes. This terrible event became known as 'The Big Die Up'.

At about the same time as 'The Big Die Up', the U.S. railroad network was extended. Track was laid over the routes of the cattle trails, so cattle no longer had to be driven from Texas to the northern states. The cowboy's most important job, driving cattle, disappeared. Cowboys permanently settled on the ranches as ranch hands.

Today, people still work in the cattle business. But modern technology has made their jobs easier, safer – and perhaps less exciting. But the legend of the cowboy lives on, in memory of the 40,000 young men who, between the 1860's and 1880's, spent their lives driving cattle north from Texas.

Cowboy Slang

bardog	bartender
bear sign	doughnuts
bone orchard	cemetery
broomtail	unbroken horse
bug juice	whiskey or other hard liquor
bunkie	partner
bushwacked	shot from ambush
cavvy	saddle horse not in use, part of the remuda
chouse	stir up, get moving
cinch	sure thing
critter	any animal
dust cutter	drink
featherhead	stupid person
fourflusher	bluffer
goose-drowner	cloudburst
hayshaker	farmer (also **hen wrangler**)
honkytonk	saloon
hightail it	depart rapidly
heeled	armed
keep cases	watch
loco	crazy
nester	small farmer
nighthawk	man in charge of herd at night
on the prod	fighting mad
ornery	bad tempered
rimrocker	tireless horse
runt	puny calf or foal
redeye	whiskey or other alcoholic drink
shebang	way station, dilapidated building, the the whole thing
pronto	right now
sucamagrowl	sweet pudding or pie
warbag	cowboy's personal luggage
vamoose	scram
yack	talk a lot
yellow	cowardly

Index

Answers for page 12
1. Bar Z Bar 2. Broken Arrow 3. X Bar Two
4. Barbeque 5. Forty or Four D 6. Apple
7. Diamond 8. Half Diamond
9. Diamond and a Half 10. Four Sixes
11. Triple K 12. Triple K Connected 13. Anchor
14. Rocking K 15. Bow and Arrow 16. Walking A
17. Too Hot 18. Flower Pot 19. Flying Heart
20. Broken Heart 21. Sunrise 22. Box